Social Media Marketing Productivity Hacks

Beat Procrastination And Sell More By Using Time Management Strategies And Tools To Help Your Business Grow on Instagram, YouTube, Facebook And More in 2020

By Rory Ames-Hyatt

Table of Contents

which are incurred as a result of the use of the information contained within this document, including, but not limited to errors, omissions, or inaccuracies.

Introduction

Look around you.

There has been a change in the way we communicate. At one point, you could watch advertisements on television. The radio showed you quick snippets of promotions. Magazines showed models and products to you as you browsed their pages.

Not today.

You could be practically anywhere in the world. You could be flying at 31,000 feet. You could be viewing a mobile device in a movie theatre, much to everyone'?s chagrin. Or perhaps, you are on a boat out at sea.

In all of these locations, you can be bombarded with marketing promotions.

Today, you are more connected than ever. Through social media, you are never too far away from the next marketing campaign. In fact, one could say you are quite literally face-to-face with an advertisement.

However, with the advent of newer technologies for social media marketing, we need new tools. We need tools to help us manage our marketing efforts. We need tools for time management and effective teamwork. But we do not need these tools for large scale organizations. We need to provide these tools for small-scale businesses, entrepreneurs, and freelancers.

That is what you will find in this book.

You will find a lot of convenient platforms for creating ideas, for communicating with your team, for storage and time management; you will find them all here.

So as they say, without further ado, let us dive in.

1 Growth of Social Media

Social media marketing was born with the need to reach a growing number of people. Brands wanted to reach out to more people in new ways. Unlike television, newspapers, and other advertising mediums, you can personalize your messages on social media. With that being said, if you could reach the right target audience, you had a better chance to make a sale. And not just for the revenues. Brands started using social networking to address concerns, communicate with the audience, and build brand value and loyalty.

It was a virtually untapped market. But thanks to the growing number of users, businesses could no longer ignore the huge potential of social media marketing.

It can arguably be said that social media marketing, or advertising, started with Facebook launching '?Pages' in 2007. Brands, for the first time, were able to have a presence on the network. They could build their audience and convert them into customers. A new term was born—'cost per fan.' This received a further boost when Facebook allowed paid advertising. This form of advertising was tweaked over time to make the system even better.

Now, there is a demographic matching, marketplace, and a lot more features to make Facebook advertising very efficient. Twitter, too, launched the '?Promoted Tweet' in 2010. Instagram, Snapchat, Pinterest, and LinkedIn all have their advertising products now that businesses can use for promotions.

Today, you will find almost every business on social media—?from large multinational conglomerates to the neighborhood grocery store. Successful businesses are using social media marketing for lead generation, research, branding, customer retention, and e-commerce. New businesses and brands are launched on Facebook and on the other networks, revealing future plans and making announcements. Advertising, video, live streaming, demographic matching, and technology upgrades are some forms of technology available for businesses. These features help businesses find new and improved ways to reach out and market their brands.

Many businesses today adopt social media marketing to grant them a wider audience, better promotional capabilities, and the power of incredible reach. Gone are the days of spending enormous sums of money setting up billboards and hoping that your target audience will see them. Moreover, traditional forms of marketing do have the capacity to provide businesses with detailed insights. Everything seems rather arbitrary. How many people actually saw the billboard and reacted to it? Could businesses have paid the same amount and reached people through better means? Through social media, the time required to market services and products has been significantly reduced.

Customer service has improved. 83 percent of customers posting complaints on a website, like Twitter, receive a quick reply. With this, the overall customer satisfaction is also improved. Businesses are thus able to retain customers better.

80 percent of the US population is on social media. It's much the same everywhere in the Western and the developing or the developed world. 53 percent of people on social media are following a brand, but the popularity of social media and the impact on marketing is expected to be even greater in the next few years. With the growth of mobile technology, one can expect the reach of social advertising to increase tremendously. There was a time when owning a mobile gadget means shelling out big bucks to get cool features. However, these days

you have manufacturers creating phones with incredible features at a portion of the cost of big-branded phones.

So, what is going to be the future of social media marketing? What are the emerging technologies, user habits, trends, and new features? How are businesses going to adapt to the changing world to boost their social media presence and marketing activities?

1 Uses of Social Media

Getting Access to New Customers

There are billions of people around the world using some type of social platform or even multiple platforms. It has become a way for people to share and communicate with their friends on just about anything. There are swarms of new customers waiting on your business. They would talk about it, especially if they had a good experience with your products and services.

Customers or potential customers will also speak negatively about your business if they have had a bad experience. As a local business owner, you must have a plan in place for complaints. Many of the larger businesses like to engage and take care of customer issues on places like Twitter because of the convenience and ease of the platform.

As of September 2013, 72 percent of online adults were using social networking sites, according to the Pew Research Center. This is happening over just about every demographic regardless of circumstances. In addition, social media campaigns are more effective in generating quality leads. This information spells out the opportunity for local businesses.

Building and Engaging with Potential Customers

I can't express enough about the importance of building your audience first. Consumers won't buy much, if any at all, when they do not get your attention. There are many ways of doing this, such as sharing great content about your products or by asking questions.

"Great content" may throw some of you off a bit, but it's simple and here's an example. Let's say you have a bakery business in your town or city and you have an Instagram page. You already have one thousand plus followers for the page. That means a fair number of people will see your posts organically. You could use this to communicate more about your delightful baked goodies. You could also discuss the history of your products and how it came about, as an example. When users comment on your posts, be sure to respond and answer their questions if needed. Your customers or potential customers love to be engaged with and valued. In this way, you can use the platform to build trust with your customers.

Show Up in the Search Results

When you set up social profiles, some may show in the search results. The search results occur on search engines like Google, Bing, and Yahoo. This is important because you gain more awareness and direction people toward your products and services. Notice the URL bar (the box that shows "http://www.......com"), and look at the name of the user, which is typically found after the "....com/social-username." After you add your business name, chances are that your profile may appear in the search results when you begin social media marketing. This is a great way of getting organic traffic to your social media profile with a little ingenuity on your part.

You Can Access the Power of Mobile

Some business owners can easily be confused when they try to understand what mobile technology can really do for them. This is because they are told and pitched heavily on mobile apps.

Local businesses are searched for heavily on social media sites, such as Facebook, Twitter, Pinterest, and even Instagram, with mobile devices. The thing to remember is that your social media profiles within these platforms. Your profiles must be set up properly to enable geo or location features within those mobile platforms.

A local business can also benefit from many other features from a mobile platform. You can easily integrate with social media, including email marketing and text messaging. You can use QR codes, mobile-optimized social campaigns (contests, surveys & games), and mobile coupons. The true benefit of mobile is that all of these benefits can be tracked for performance. This way, you can see all the available data and make conscious decisions overall.

The uses can seem endless when mobile is implemented properly with social media. Mobile cannot be ignored any longer, so position your local business now and don'?t wait to benefit from it. You can be the exception amongst your competitors in your local area. Learning how valuable mobile is supplies a great addition to your entire social media marketing strategy.

Chapter 1: Why Productivity Is Key to Maximizing the ROI of Your Social Media Marketing Efforts

Many companies are doing very well with social media marketing these days. The perception is that only the big brands can succeed in this new wave of marketing, but that is a common misconception.

Any small business with a simple game plan can succeed in social media marketing. This is because it's much easier to manage expectations in your local market. Social media allows you to scale your business'?s marketing efforts. The competition in your local area is much, much lower. In fact, it doesn't matter if you are a local bakery in a city with 100 other bakeries, your chances of being visible with social media marketing are high in your own "backyard." Here's why: a large number of local businesses using social media aren'?t doing it right.

Your customers are using social media and are likely also using many other social platforms. Your business has potential customers looking for it within these different platforms, and you can reach them at minimal cost.

In fact, you could save a lot of money using social media marketing.

There are a few reasons for this.

1). Internet Access Is Spreading Rapidly

Wherever you decide to locate your business in the world, you can "connect" with your customers. Internet access is becoming simpler by the second and making social media accessible. That might not be a revelation, but as a small business owner, you have to recognize and adapt to it.

More and more people - even in remote areas - are gaining internet access. Fiber optics and satellite internet services are technologies making this possible. This is happening all over the world with high frequency. With internet access, your customers are a click away from you. They can look for your products and services anywhere, and at any time.

What's more, you can reach out to them, as well. You can perform effective customer service through your social platforms. You can even make sales happen! Most consumers are comfortable with businesses in their own communities, which is why reaching out to them is not that difficult. It only requires a strong social presence.

2). The Mobile Wave Is Here to Stay

Mobile is getting bigger by the minute. Think of all the smartphones available in the market. You have high-end models with a rather high price tag, and then you have cheaper alternatives packed with a lot of features.

With this, you have people across the globe connected via a mobile device. According to Statista, the world'?s mobile population reached 3.7 billion users in a January 2018 data collection. That's almost half the world's population. In other words, every other person on the planet has a mobile device.

Mobile marketing can be beneficial for your business and has the power to take it to another level. Your customers have mobile devices and are using them all the time. One might even say that it consumes their identity to a degree.

We need and cherish our mobile devices. We depend on them for just about everything because of convenient services and apps. Many people spend countless hours on their mobile devices using social media sites.

Local business owners would never imagine the importance of mobile marketing as a way to catapult their business. "Social is Mobile and Mobile is Local," is the motto here. You can't have one without the other if you want to compete locally.

Social media sites, such as Facebook, Twitter, Instagram, Periscope, Snapchat, WhatsApp, and even Pinterest, have location-based features. With these features, users can find you even as they pass by your place of business.

You practically have a two-pronged attack opportunity. One, you can use marketing to reach out to users. Secondly, you can make yourself visible to nearby people.

That is what social media gives you: the power to be aware.

3). Modern-Day Distribution Is Incredible

Thirty years ago, distribution with just about any medium was way too expensive. Publishing a book, distributing any news source, etc. were all expensive endeavors. It was nearly impossible to do these things on a budget. Fast forward to current times, and you will see that it's unbelievably accessible.

I like to categorize distribution into four categories: easy, free, cheap, and targeted.

Easy

These days, all you need is internet access and a PC or mobile device. With just a social platform and an identity, you are ready to start selling or promoting. There are many social media sites to access nowadays. They are very easy to use, as well.

Free

Distributing content is free when you use social media to share with an audience. Thus, this accessibility is far more effective.

There is one fact that many people share in this world; free is good. Most people will opt to use a free tool they can sign up for by providing simple information. With social media, such a process is available.

Cheap

This is the one where I always get a reaction of, "?Huh?" Yes... cheap! Distribution of content can be cheap when using for marketing purposes. You can see this in PPC or pay-per-click advertising on social media sites. In a pay-per-click advertising model, you only pay when you receive clicks on your ad. Two of the most effective social media sites for that are Facebook and YouTube. And on these platforms, it is not very expensive to use PPS advertising.

Targeted

The most exciting part of distributing content in current times is the ability to target. As a business owner, only you know who your customers are. After using the analytics from a few of your social media sites, you know how to reach your customers. In some cases, you will be able to pinpoint exactly where to find these customers, as well.

Now, you might think that with all this connectivity, your task is now easy. You just need to bombard people will your promotions and voila! Instant awareness. You can almost imagine the sound of the cash register!

But the reality is different. You see, it is one thing to reach out to people, yet it is quite another to make that reach profitable. You could have thousands of people see your social media ads, but what is the point if only 30 people show up at your business location?

This is where productivity comes in.

Time for a crash course.

In business, productivity is simply the difference between input and output. Basically, how much do you put into your efforts to generate a desired result? It is an indication of the efficiency in a process.

Now, let's try seeing how productivity helps you, both in your business and in social media marketing:

Your process will be efficient.

Worrying about why it takes time to get things done? Now you know. Having a productive mindset lets you accomplish more, but the difference is that you will be generating quality output.

You can accomplish more.

Time is money. In business, that is not a philosophical quote, it is a principle. So with having the right influx of productivity, you can complete more tasks within the time you have.

Accomplishing more means more money.

Once again, time is money. When more tasks get done, you are on the track to completing more sales orders. And more sales bring in more dollars in the bank.

Group morale.

It is all about teamwork these days. However, if you are the only one putting in effort, what is the point of teamwork? Productivity increases group morale and that, in return, improves output.

Customer expectations.

At the end of the day, you need to keep customers satisfied. You need them to return to you. That happens if you have high-quality products. With increased productivity, you keep your products or services in the best quality. This has a wonderful effect on customer expectations; they begin to expect the best from you.

You save money.

You need to pay your employees. That becomes part of your expenses. However, through productivity, you get more output for the same time. Your employees are paid the same, but they give out more. That saves money. Think of it this way, imagine your employees are generating less for the same salary. Technically, your cost of production has increased.

You and your team can have a personal life.

Your team needs to stay motivated. So do you. A lack of personal life will only serve to demotivate you and everyone else. Through productive work, you get tasks done on time. This leaves time for extracurricular activities and allow you to tend to your personal affairs.

Sense of accomplishment.

If there is a lack of progress, then everyone feels the pressure of disappointment. Every business should show progress, however big or small it is. By completing things on time, you feel a sense of accomplishment. This motivates your team to work harder.

You meet deadlines.

In the corporate world these days, every goal has a deadline. If your productivity is low, you cannot reach those deadlines. Every deadline missed is an opportunity lost. Every opportunity is a potential to make money.

Meeting demands.

At the end of the day, customer demands have to be met. When you know that the market has more demand for your product, why produce less? Realize that customer demands do not exist for long. They eventually wane and dissipate. You only get one opportunity to make the most out of it.

Chapter 2: The Mindset of Productivity (And How to Cultivate That Mindset)

Plan your day.

The first thing you have to do is to plan your day. You need to keep your goals realistic and well-defined. It is wonderful to think that you want to create a profit of a million dollars, but that is not your daily plan.

What are your tasks for the day?

What small goals have you set for yourself and your team?

How do you accomplish things?

You ask these questions after taking stock of where you are. You want that million dollars. What are you going to do every day to get to that point?

Know your customers.

This may seem far-fetched, but knowing your customers is important. If you cannot define your customers, you will be working hard for the wrong reasons.

Many businesses have started and failed not because their product or their marketing efforts were bad, but because they were going after the wrong customers. When marketing, remember to focus on your customers and their needs, not your product or service. People don't care about a product or its perks. They care about how they can benefit from what you have. And you need to realize that your audience is intelligent. They don't want hype; they want the truth. The more you hype, the more they will be looking for the catch. So if you give them the honest statement right away, they will stop looking for it, and they will begin to trust you.

Remember, you have to listen to what your customers have to say. You have to understand what they are really looking for, which is why you cannot have a real target market.

Eventually, you will know who you are reaching out to. Your work begins to reap results. You see the effect of your productivity and you take steps to better yourself.

Do not waste time on how good your product or service is.

Keep your "me," "I," "?my," "our," and "mine" to a minimum. Instead, focus your marketing approach on "you" and "yours."

Try this exercise. Check how you have written out your marketing pitch. Check how many times you use "?I," "my," "our," or "mine." Now, compare it to how many times you use "you" and "your." The latter should far outweigh the former.

With this, you will have an easier time reaching your customers. Your productivity is focused in the right direction. You begin to keep customers.

Get good at getting personal.

Make sure you speak to an individual rather than an audience. People want to feel like you'?re talking directly to them. The really smart marketers speak to *one* person.

One version is a speech, as talking to an audience.

"As you know."

"You might be aware."

These are common forms of speech to connect with your audience.

Another version you can use is a conversation. People are much more willing to be invested in a conversation than in a presentation.

Through a personal connection, you will know how to plan your marketing efforts. This will help you plan your daily actions. This helps you increase your productivity.

Build the trust.

The more you build up a relationship with people on things they can relate to, the more trust they have. The more they trust you, the more they're willing to come back. And this means they're willing to spend more on you to improve their lives.

Building trust is important for a very particular reason. When you build trust, you will need to spend less effort on promotions. That gives you more time to spend on business growth. Your productivity multiplies as you receive more time for strategic decisions. You benefit from this. Your business benefits from this. Eventually, your time begins to make money.

l Social Media Entrepreneur'?s ABC

There are a few things you can do to improve productivity on social media.

Large brands with huge advertising budgets have deep pockets to spend considerably on marketing. For entrepreneurs who have just started their business, every penny would make a big difference. When such is the case, social media plays a crucial role in acting as the free marketing and business scaling tool.

Every entrepreneur starts his or her business hoping to scale it up in the near future. To scale the business, one would most definitely look to gain sufficient traction. Social media acts as an important tool in garnering traction.

An ambitious entrepreneur such as yourself might start a business and would look at marketing the business. Let us assume that you don't possess a boatload of money. You might not go for televised advertisements or newspaper advertisements. Word-of-mouth marketing would probably be your consideration. However, it isn't possible to verbally communicate to a billion people at the same time. Since the people you seek to market are already virtually connected, social media is becoming the savior under such circumstances. With a billion connected, social media marketing is just an enhanced version of word-of-mouth marketing. Rather than orally telling a billion people, you draft creative posts and content to capture their attention. Thereby, you end up propagating your business.

The entire point of marketing is to reach out to people. The more people you reach out to, the more people you can inform about your products and services.

Step 1: Craft a Clear Objective

The first step to marketing using social media is to have a clear objective. You have to have a crystal clear objective of what you want social media to do. Is it to raise followers and increase the engagement you receive on your social platform? If it'?s an app, is it to increase the number of users? Is it to generate more user activity for a website or is it to generate business leads? The objective need not necessarily be quantifiable objectives. Although, a quantifiable objective would be most helpful. This is so you know the extent of success your campaign has accumulated.

A clear objective lets you know if the money you spend is adhering to the plan. It also lets you know if the plan you have is working. These short term business goals must be in concurrence with the long term goals to establish overall business clarity.

Step 2: Research Your Market

The more time you invest in researching your market, the better the plan execution will be. It's very important to study the mindset of your target audience. Their mindset is what will ultimately lead them to ignore a post or share it amongst their circle. Your marketing efforts can also be focused. The content could be drafted keeping the target audience in mind.

Spending time analyzing the market for areas of weakness and areas of strength would most certainly give insight. You would find out about the opportunities where your business will have the best chance to grow.

Step 3: Craft the Creative

Once you have the target audience, the next step would be to draft creative content that would capture their attention. There is a thin line between ignoring a post and sharing or retweeting a post.

Billions of posts crowd the timeline, be it Facebook or Twitter. At the end of the day, a footnote mention here or there depends on the quality of the post. As you scroll down your timeline, you will notice a major chunk of them being useless posts. You would invariably end up getting frustrated when looking at the huge chunk of spam.

Hence, fine-tuning the post to the taste of the target audience could serve to be more effective.

Step 4: Optimizing for the Masses

This is the part where the social media trending tool can be put to use. "?#Trending" is a type of label used on social media to categorize posts. When the whole world is talking about the "#Superbowl," the "#Superbowl" label would be trending. This is because of the sheer volume of mentions. It makes it easier for users to find messages with a specific theme or content. Additionally, you get to share conversations with a lot of people who share the same interests. This is effective for reaching out to a specific group of people.

Such trending topics could be addressed by your posts. This could create a large viewership and post activity, thereby driving engagement. After all, engagement is what we are aiming for.

Step 5: Business Alliances and Partnerships

The idea of business alliances and partnerships could be formal or informal. Social media allows you to form informal business alliances or partnerships. You can do this by joining groups or pages of common interest. These groups or pages keep you up to date on the topics you follow. It could also generate new business leads, as those in the group are like-minded, possessing similar interests.

Are you posting on the right platform and posting engaging content? If so, you will definitely be viewed as a social media expert. Being at the right place at the right time with the right content allows you to scale your business.

Step 6: Measure the Metrics

The power of a good story always involves a plot made up of numbers. Numbers make or break a story and can be used to manipulate and obfuscate the narrative.

Through numbers, the performance metrics tell us if you are on the right track. It lets you know if you are where you pictured yourself to be. They make us adhere to the plan and ensure that our objectives are met in the end. Such metrics in marketing are the number of likes, shares, reaches, and the click-through rate in social media. Numbers do tell us a tale, and it's up to us to lend our ears.

Social Media: To Infinity and Beyond

Generating leads is the most crucial part for the majority of businesses, hence the reason why they maintain a social media presence. This eventually improves your productivity.

The more fans, the merrier the business, as the reach would be immense. The better the reach, the greater the potential to generate good business leads.

If you have something to say, no matter who you are, the content has to be worth hearing. Social media is incredibly useful in promoting this content, but without good content, your efforts are in vain. Your content just gets flooded into an ocean of spam. To make your efforts bear fruits, you need to be conscious of what your target audience wants. This means interacting with them on a day-to-day basis to captivate their mindset.

When you post something online, the content needs to engage the followers. Every step is about creating value, and value creation does not come easy. You need to remember that it's not just about getting the message across. Engaging the followers and promoting the brand is an art in itself. It's all about creating a good experience in the end. A customer with a good reading or shopping experience would promote the content or the service. Such is the power of experience. Creating a good experience will tend to work in your favor for building your brand and expanding your reach.

Chapter 3: Productivity Tools for YouTube

YouTube is, without a doubt, a major force in the content marketing plans for the day. And that is unlikely to change anytime soon. There are currently more than 1.3 billion registered users on YouTube. At least 70 percent of those create content in one fashion or another for the site. Current studies estimate that more than 75 percent of all of the traffic on the internet is video. More than half of all web traffic after 9 pm is video traffic from Netflix and YouTube primarily.

Video plays such an important role in social media marketing of all types. The importance of having a strong online video presence is only going to continue to increase as time goes on. From a marketing standpoint, YouTube provides content creators the opportunity to form a real connection with the viewer. It allows you to really explain the ins and outs of the product or service being provided. It allows you to share news. You can give information. When done correctly, the average viewer will be a converted customer. He or she will be a profitable pair of eyes on additional videos, as well.

We have covered the basics of YouTube. Let us look at some productivity apps for the platform.

1 YouTube Creator Studio

The Creator studio - recently renamed to YouTube Studio - is a tool on YouTube. It is a powerful tool to organize your videos. You can also interact with fans and dive into your analytics.

With its recent version, there have been a few additions:

1. There are three new metrics in the analytics section. These

are impressions, unique viewers, and impression click-through rates.

2. You receive personalized news and information. This is to help you with your channel.

Now why are these updates useful? Let's break them down one by one.

New Metrics

With new metrics, you will be able to better understand your video. Impressions show you the number of times viewers have seen your thumbnail. This allows you to know the potential reach of your videos.

Using impression click-through rates, you can find out how many impressions turned to views. This is important to know if your thumbnails are working or your captions are interesting. Alternatively, you can find out if people are interested in your content.

The third metric, unique viewers, lets you see the number of different people who watched your content. Through this, you will find out original viewers versus repeated viewings.

Personalized News and Information

These are there to give you more relevant information about your videos. For example, let us assume you are posting videos about cars. You will receive relevant videos about car parts, latest cars, vehicle mods, etc. These are there to help you curate content for your video or to just simply give you inspiration.

l Benefits of YouTube Studio

If you have a YouTube channel, then this is the tool you should have. Think of it like your point of entry to your content.

Let us see why this tool is preferred by virtually all content creators:

1. You can easily organize your videos. Want to update your video? Sure. Need to change thumbnails of multiple videos? Of course. Need some settings altered - like video size - for a few of your videos? You can do that here. You have complete control over how your videos are presented to your audience.

2. Here is a question to think about: If you have uploaded your videos, how do you know how well they are performing? Are views enough to gauge a video'?s popularity? How can you truly measure the interest between two or more videos? You need insights, and that's what YouTube Studio gives you. You can receive in-depth insights about your video. This allows you to fine-tune your content and keep it relevant.

3. Let us assume your videos are gaining popularity. You are receiving tons of comments! Whoa! How do you handle them? Are you going to have to manually go into a video and respond? Calm down there. YouTube Studio allows you to manage comments in one space.

4. Okay, so you are not a professional music editor. You do not have software. But your videos need that "?oomph" to it. Well, YouTube Studio allows you to add audio tracks to your video, making it stand out.

l The Best Feature

I love insights. I need to know how what is making my audience tick. Do people see my video thumbnail and just scroll by? What percentage of my video do people watch? This allows me to know when people leave my video. Perhaps this or that point is not interesting. Maybe my video is long.

Analytics is such a powerful tool to make sure your content is interesting. Without analytics, it'?s like firing in a dark room and hoping you land your shots.

It is important to pay attention to your channel as it is essentially the homepage tying any, and all, of your disparate content together into one easy-to-explore place. Remember, every video that ends up on your YouTube channel is another opportunity to improve site traffic. Every video ultimately points back to the channel page and starts the process all over again.

l VidIQ

This tool is a Google Chrome extension. It basically allows you to view data about other people'?s videos on YouTube. Think you got a competitor who is doing better than you? Find out why. Or, you could be inspired by a particular YouTube channel, wanting to find out what makes them popular.

The most important feature of this tool, however, is its capability to optimize your own videos.

l Benefits of VidIQ

Here is why this tool has been gaining popularity in recent times:

1. Typically, you cannot use YouTube Studio to see insights into other creators'? accounts. But what if you want to check out what they do right? Enter, VidIQ. While it may not provide you with all the details as does YouTube Studio, it is still useful. You can make actionable decisions based on your new information.
2. You may probably know about YouTube SEO. You can find tons of websites giving you SEO tips. But with VidIQ, you can find out just exactly what you need to change. No more arbitrary information. Now you know exactly where you are lacking.
3. Let us assume you are running a promotion. Now, you have

added a text that says, "?Buy our merchandise here." Let us not assume that the promotion has ended and you would remove the text. If you have more than 100 videos, that would be a tedious task! But with VidIQ, you can remove specific texts from multiple videos. Neat, huh?

4. One of the best features is that you can discover popular and relevant tags for your videos. Not only that, but you can also find out what tags others are using in their videos. With this knowledge, you can perfect your video'?s SEO.

l The Best Feature

Believe me when I say this, manually editing your video descriptions is such a tedious task. The idea of removing content with just one click is truly helpful. No more endless click into video, edit, save, and exit. Now it is just click, delete, and it is done!

l TubeBuddy

TubeBuddy is a browser extension that adds more features to your YouTube. It adds a menu to your YouTube account, giving you access to a horde of features.

l Benefits of TubeBuddy

1. If you need to find relevant tags for your account, you got them right here. Simply search and add.
2. What if you would like to publish your videos on Facebook, as well? If you have a Facebook page, this tool allows you to post your videos there natively. This saves the time where you have to manually upload videos to Facebook!
3. Let's say you want to find the best description or tags among a list of ideas you have. Is there a way you can find out which

one is the best? Well, this tool allows you to A/B test your titles, descriptions, tags and even your thumbnails. With this, you can see which combination of the above four parameters fit your video.

4. This is a feature that is a nifty addition. You can practically create a GIF of a part of your video, which is really useful if you are also managing a blog or other social platforms.

5. You can also check out how well your competitors are performing. It is like keeping a scorecard. If they perform better, they get certain points. You find out what they are doing better and when to improve your videos!

l The Best Feature

It is important to know which titles, descriptions, and other parameters work for your video. But how can we find that out? This is where the A/B testing feature is truly useful. This is especially true if you feel like you have so many creative ideas, but do not know which one might work.

Chapter 4: Productivity Tools for Facebook

Facebook is a platform that everyone is familiar with. When someone talks about social media marketing, assume they are definitely including Facebook on that list. That is because Facebook offers flexibility. You have tons of features and a lot of ways to reach your audience.

When you realize that many of your customers are on Facebook, you realize the potential of the platform. You know you can reach millions of customers easily. Within just a few clicks, you can market yourself on a global platform. This flexibility gives you unique perspectives, creative ideas, and marketing strategies to work with.

Let us look at two scenarios to highlight the above example. Let us assume you own a small bakery. You specialize in making homemade cookies that you would like to market to your potential customers. While looking at your marketing plan, you realize that most of your customers reside within your neighborhood or local area. This means you have to target customers locally. Facebook allows you to do that by selecting your area. When the area is selected, you can start promoting your products on your Facebook page.

Let us look at another scenario altogether. If you are a multinational firm, then you might have to target a larger audience. For this reason, you might choose multiple cities on Facebook to reach out to your audience. You could also select multiple countries in order to show your services to the right audience.

With this degree of flexibility, you could spend a lot of time figuring things out on Facebook. You need some tools to help you speed things up. If you are an entrepreneur or a small business, you might need to better manage your time. For this reason, here are some apps that will help you get started on Facebook.

1 Buffer

Let us say you have a Facebook business account. You are now ready to post your images, updates, and videos. You start with one, feeling excited. Then you go on to the next. Pretty soon, you are on your hundredth upload and you are thinking to yourself, "?Can this go any faster?"

Well, I can say that it can.

Meet Buffer.

The way this tool works is pretty simple. What you do is create your post on Buffer. You add your description, image, and all that jazz. Then you create your next one. This way, you create all your posts in one platform.

When you are ready, you can schedule each of these posts on a different time and date.

Easy, huh?

With all the legwork done initially, you just have to sit back and relax. Buffer will take care of the rest. It will post content on the date and at the time you specified.

But what makes this tool unique?

1 Benefits of Buffer

1. If you have multiple accounts, then you can use this tool to post on all of them. You can shift between accounts. You can even post the same post on different accounts. You know,

when you want to spread awareness within your own brand. Whatever your plans, the multiple account feature is truly convenient.

2. Now, let's say you created a bunch of posts. You just realized your next post is the most important of them all. Do you have to delete all your previous posts now? Not quite. You see, Buffer gives you the option to choose a specific post and publish it next. With its "?Share Next" feature, you do not have to worry about jumping the queue.

3. Insights are important, but you need to know how posting from Buffer makes a difference, so the platform gives you its own analytics. This allows you to see how the posts you published from Buffer perform. Pretty cool.

l The Best Feature

I know a lot of people have a bunch of Facebook accounts to manage. On Facebook, you have to sign out, sign back into a new account, and then manage your posts. With Buffer, you can organize all your accounts in one place.

This is useful for quickly publishing or scheduling multiple posts on multiple accounts. The amount of time you save through this is very noticeable.

l Hootsuite

Hootsuite is a popular social media management system. What this means is that you control many aspects of your social media. It gives you a bird'?s-eye view of your social media channels. You can perform social monitoring functions. You can see what people are saying about your brand. And when you want to, you can swoop in and respond.

l Benefits of Hootsuite

1. You can manage multiple accounts. This means you can manage Facebook, Instagram, Twitter, Google+, and other social accounts. This becomes particularly useful when your strategy focuses on multiple platforms. But what if you have multiple pages on the same platform? Let us assume you have two different businesses and they are both on Facebook. What about them? Will you require another Hootsuite account to add a new Facebook page? That seems rather complicated. For that reason, you can choose to add multiple pages of the same account. You can add all your Facebook pages and start working on them simultaneously.

2. Now, let us take another scenario. Let us imagine that you have a whole team of people who are working on your Facebook page. Through this, you have a person responsible for graphics. Another individual taking care of advertising. Yet another member working on your social posts. What can you do to share the team's work? Thankfully, Hootsuite provides you with a solution. You can share Hootsuite with them. This allows them to work with you on your platform. You can use the platform to delegate tasks with your team. You can communicate with your team on the platform. You can assign what tasks can be altered by which member. Additionally, you can monitor what changes your team is making. It gives you so much control over your work and allows you to effectively plan your strategy.

3. We love free stuff. Which is why, if you are using Hootsuite, you get free reports in your email. This is convenient when you are using your business email. You do not need to go to Facebook for insights. Now, you can see details about your page while answering your next mail.

4. You can schedule your posts on Hootsuite. While you are looking through your channels, you have the ability to post

on them. You even have response templates. This means that if you notice a complaint, you do not have to type a response. You can keep a specific response ready and use it instantly.

l The Best Feature

They say teamwork is key. I know that in a lot of organizations, it is never a one-man show. In such cases, getting your entire team together on one platform is truly convenient. Additionally, you can monitor your team. Talk to them. Send them reminders and create schedules for them. All in all, it is one superb package to have.

l Dlvr.it

We have not one, not two, but three awesome productivity tools. Let us move on to Dlvr.it. This is another popular automation tool for you to use. Apart from scheduling your posts, you get some other cool features you can take advantage of. One of the best features of this platform is that it is perfect for individuals. When you do not have a large team, Dlvr.it provides you with simplicity. This means you can use the platform by yourself. This means you can be a marketing team all on your own, easily scheduling posts and watching their progress.

l Benefits of Dlvr.it

1. Scheduling posts can take up much of your time. For this reason, Dlvr.it provides you with a lot of convenience for publishing your Facebook posts. You can easily schedule our posts on your Facebook page using this tool. Queue up your posts and then watch them get published on time.
2. If you have articles you would like to publish on Facebook, you can do that with Dlvr.it. If you have other forms of media, such as photos or videos, Dlvr.it can take care of that as well.

3. The platform also makes it easy to reuse your content. By reusing content, you do not have to spend time creating content from scratch. This is effective in showing that you are active on Facebook. Your customers view this in a positive light and you eventually draw more traffic. Using this, you can even attract more traffic to your website, should you have one.

4. As with Hootsuite, if you have multiple Facebook pages, you can easily link them to Dlvr.it. Once they are linked, you can begin publishing content on the platforms. Should you wish to share one single content across all platforms, you can do so as well.

5. If you have tracking features in your links, you can use them here. Link Dlvr.it to your Google Analytics account and get link insights.

6. Here is the best part. You can give access to your website'?s RSS feed and Dlvr.it will take care of the rest. Using your feed, it will automatically post on your social media platforms.

l *The Best Feature*

The RSS feed, hands down. Think about it. You have an e-commerce company and you are constantly updating your site. What better way to send across your updates than through Dlvr.it. I mean, you do not even have to create posts. Sure, you will have limited creative control if you use this method, but you can still just shoot out quick updates, keeping your audience informed.

Chapter 5: Productivity Tools for Instagram

If you have been uploading images or videos recently, chances are you have been doing it on Instagram. This tool exploded into the scene in 2010. Ever since then, it has gone through many changes. Some good, some not so good. Either way, it has established a foothold in the marketing world. Everyone, from Nike to Coca-Cola to even the banking sector, use this platform. Let us see if we can't get some cool productivity tools for this platform.

According to recent statistics, there are close to 800 million people on Instagram. Out of these, more than 500 million people use the platform every day. This goes to show the platform'?s influence in people's lives.

Instagram is a wonderful tool for sharing media. You can combine images, videos, and even slideshows to effectively communicate any message you would like. What makes Instagram so demanded is that any form of business can thrive on the platform. You could be a large-scale organization and still be able to use Instagram for your business. Mercedes-Benz and Aston Martin are global companies utilizing the platform for their benefit. You could even be a local store and use Instagram to market yourself. There are numerous accounts belonging to people who have a skill they would like to market. In this way, even individuals can create a market for their talents on Instagram.

Another feature Instagram offers is the opportunity to partner up with influencers. This means you can use someone who has a small or big group of following to market your product. Or, you can use them to talk about your services.

Alternatively, you can be an influencer yourself. You could use the platform to reach out to an audience of like-minded people.

With all of these features, you require a tool that can easily take care of your publishing requirements.

1 Tailwind

Tailwind is a marketing tool specifically created for Instagram and Pinterest. It is perfect for bloggers and small businesses. It can also be used by influencers who are starting out their journey, as it simplifies the social media marketing process. When you are new to Instagram marketing, you can use this tool to easily navigate the marketing process. You can reach out to your followers without much hassle. Through using this tool, you can easily schedule posts, discover content, and track conversations.

1 Benefits of Tailwind

1. You can easily schedule content for Instagram. This allows you to get everything done in one go so you can go back to your other tasks.
2. You receive detailed insights and analytics for your posts. This is convenient when you want to monitor your posts'? effectiveness. Through this, you can even choose which post to use for paid promotion. As Instagram's paid promotion is slightly more expensive than Facebook's, this feature is useful. You will not spend unnecessary money on your platform.
3. You can check the latest trends and activities on Instagram. This is useful when you want to get some ideas for your content.
4. When someone comments on your Instagram content, you can view them and respond. With this, you do not have to

manually select a comment like you would on Instagram. Simply post your response through an effective pop-up.

5. You can set up KPIs for yourself and monitor them. This allows you to see if you have reached your goals on the social platform. By doing this, you can decide if you are satisfied with the current strategy. If you are not, you can change them completely.

l The Best Feature

Most businesses have goals to achieve. It is how they monitor performance. It is the way to keep track of progress. With Tailwind'?s KPI monitoring feature, making sure you are heading in the right direction becomes really easy. You practically have full control over your Instagram marketing strategies, budget, and creatives.

l SocialBlade

While Instagram is an effective tool for marketing, it takes time to build your reputation. This is partly because competition is high on the platform. You go up against some of the most creative Instagram business accounts out there.

In the world of social media, analytics are powerful. Knowing is the key to making informed decisions. With the right statistics, you can decide how much you would like to spend on the platform. You can focus on seeing the results of your work. Let us assume you have been posting on Instagram for a while. You notice some of your posts get less likes than others. Some receive more comments. But is that then the only way to see if your posts are actually performing better? What if you are getting a lot of views on a post, but not a lot of comments? That could mean people like your post, but do not feel compelled to comment on it.

Moreover, by tracking analytics, you save time figuring out what to do next. You may have a strategy that might not be working well. Using analytics, you can see exactly where you are going wrong. You can also find out what you have been doing right.

Remember, it is more important to reach out to people initially than to attract more comments. Your aim should be to market yourself properly. The likes and comments will follow soon after. While that is something you can handle, you still need to know how your Instagram is performing, which is why you have SocialBlade.

l Benefits of Using SocialBlade

1. It is not easy to get detailed analytics for Instagram. There are many platforms out there that can offer you analytical features. SocialBlade, however, is one of the detailed ones you can find. With this tool, you compare yourself to other brands. Find out what is trending in your industry and get some cool ideas. You can even find out who is doing well in your community.

2. You can see who is gaining real followers and who is not. Let us assume you have a competitor who posted two posts last week. Both posts received no interactions. Yet, somehow, he or she gained 4,000 followers in just two days. How did this happen? With SocialBlade, you can keep a check on your competitors easily.

3. Additionally, you can see which accounts follow and then unfollow. Basically, some accounts follow people, and as soon as they receive followers, they unfollow them. By using SocialBlade, you can find out which accounts use these tactics.

l The Best Feature

I want to know how my competitors are doing, so if someone gains a lot of followers in a short period of time, I want to know why. SocialBlade gives me that knowledge, and you know what they say about knowledge; it is truly power. Using this, you can decide if you have to worry about your competitors, or just to check and see what they are doing right.

1 Boomerang

If you are on Instagram and you do not know about Boomerang, then you have probably been in hiding. Actually, people who do not use Instagram know what Boomerang is. This app allows you to create a short sequence of video that plays in a loop, forwards and backwards. As soon as this app was launched, creators have used it in many creative ways.

Let us look at some of its cool benefits.

1 Benefits of Boomerang

1. It allows you to create unique content for your Instagram. This content is easily consumed by audiences. When they see your Boomerang posts, their curiosity is piqued to the fullest. They want to know more about you.
2. A short burst of content that plays on a loop is eye-catching. This is because a lot of people may get bored with images. In addition to that, they may not have the time to watch an entire video. In such cases, a Boomerang comes in handy. It is short. It is interesting. It promotes your brand effectively.
3. Your creativity is the limit. The number of ways in which you can use this tool is bountiful. You can create competitions, send funny messages, use promotions, or simply have fun. Through a number of ways, you can engage with your

audience.

4. Boomerang also gives you the option to add music to your post! With this, you can create incredibly fun and vivid content for your followers.

l The Best Feature

You are in control. There is such creative potential in Boomerang. With just a short clip, you can make a powerful impact. I love how no matter what industry you are a part of, this tool can work for you. For bloggers, Boomerang is a delightful addition. You can make your content engaging, snappy, and playful.

Chapter 6: Productivity Tools for Twitter

Twitter has changed the way content is consumed. It practically removed the idea of using long pieces of text. It incorporated short updates, giving way to some incredible potential. Now, everyone from brands to movie stars to even presidents use Twitter! But with the presence of Twitter, comes the way you want to consume content. This brings us to the below apps. In order to make the best use of your time on Twitter, these apps are your choice.

Twitter is a tool that is popular with a number of people. You see politicians on Twitter. You can spot celebrities using Twitter, as well. From your favorite sporting players to your beloved authors, they all have an account on Twitter. But what makes this platform so popular?

One of the reasons people use Twitter is because it allows for an effective way to communicate with your audience. Using limited text, you can create snippets of the message you would like to say. This way, people who have little time can easily browse through the content. Additionally, you can network well on Twitter. As your tweets are public, you can be seen by potential businesses or customers. By looking at your content, they can form an impression about you. It is also much easier for you to join in on the conversation. This way, you can make your presence known or show your expertise in a field.

It has been revealed that 75% of Twitter users feel confident about small businesses after following their tweets. That statistic has a powerful impact on your business. If you are a small business owner, you have the potential to boost your awareness considerably. Three in four people are likely to form favorable impressions about your brand based on your tweets.

However, with the availability of such ease comes the task of building your profile on the platform. For small business owners, managing profiles on Twitter can be busy work. In order to make things easier, you have the following apps to help with productivity on the platform.

1 Tweetbot

If you have been using Twitter for a while, then you know you will notice a lot of content. Some of this content may be useful to you. Others may not be that important for your viewing. In such cases, you might need a filter to remove the content that is not important to you.

Tweetbot is a third party app for Twitter that gives you access to a ton of features. These features allow you to experience Twitter in a way that is comfortable to you. Let us look at these features and how they benefit us.

1 Benefits of Tweetbot

1. Tweetbot uses a filter feature. This allows you to remove certain types of tweets you do not want to see. Let us assume you have been following a particular type of content on Twitter. However, you notice some posts that are either offensive or vulgar to your taste. While this may not typically be a problem, you realize they are not exactly important. Using Tweetbot, you can easily remove this content.
2. It comes with a special dark mode. This is useful during the night, especially when you do not want to be blinded by the bright lights.
3. You can add multiple Twitter accounts, allowing you to see feeds from all of them. Switching between accounts is also made simple.
4. Unlike Twitter, Tweetbot allows you to command options

with a simple swipe. This is useful when you want to perform an action without having to click around too much.

5. One of the best features about Tweetbot is its ability to mute content. You can mute based on keywords, hashtags, and even users. This gives you the ability to look at specific content relevant for you. For businesses, you can focus on the content that gives you inspiration or the competitors you want to monitor closely. For example, let us assume that you notice a lot of content related to footwear appearing on your feed. Footwear may not be the type of content relevant for you. It becomes a hassle when you have to manually remove such content every time you see it. Hence, using Tweetbot, you can simply enter the keyword "Footwear" as the content you do not want to see. From that point onwards, all content featuring footwear will not be shown to you.

6. Insights are important and, with Tweetbot, you get some useful insights to plan your content. Through insights, you can see what content is working for you. You can check which of your tweets are reaching audiences and which are not. Using this information, you can modify your tweets. Perhaps people may not understand your tweets. Perhaps the content can be made smaller. You can analyze your tweets and figure out an effective content strategy. This way, you are able to fine-tune your tweets. Eventually, you will have a content structure and idea that works best for you.

l The Best Feature

In essence, Tweetbot allows you to curate content. This is useful for your business to discover information, ideas, or competitor approach. Posting on Tweetbot is easy and convenient, as it gives you multiple display features, too. My favorite feature, however, has to be the mute content feature. I do not want to see every bit of news on something.

Let's say I want to search on the environment. I like to know about climate change, but I do not want to be bombarded with tweets from environmental agencies. With Tweetbot, I can personalize my content and exclude information from these agencies. This allows me to see content on environment from individuals and publishers instead, giving me the kind of substance I need.

l Plume

Now that we know how to mute content, what about organizing it?

If you like a particular content or account on Twitter, you might want to see their posts more. Plume allows you to do that. This plays well with the idea that you can see the content you want to see.

Plume gives you some cool organizational features that we will take a look at below.

l Benefits of Plume

1. It gives you all the features of Twitter, plus more. You can tweet, retweet, show your love to a post, and more. With this, it feels like Plume gave Twitter a massive overhaul. It works well because you can use this platform to view Twitter content and post your own.

2. If you like a tweet, use a color on it. The next time you use Plume, that user'?s tweets will appear in that color. This allows you to easily identify a tweet. You can do this for multiple users, assigning different colors to each. Through this, you can keep a watch on those tweets that matter most to you. Let us illustrate this with an example. Say you are following a sporting magazine. You would like to identify the content from this magazine so that you do not miss out on its updates. You can use a specific color, say blue, to mark all the content

of this sporting magazine. Now, let us also assume you would like to see content from a sporting personality. It could be a famous golfer, football player, or anyone else of the kind. You can then use a different color, say green, to mark the content of this personality's Twitter account. Now that you have done the above, your content is organized effectively. Every time you spot a content highlighted in blue, you know where it is coming from. And when you spot content highlighted in green, you know it is your favorite sports person updating his or her Twitter profile.

3. What about tweets that just annoy you? Well, you can mute them. Yep, block a user or a specific content with this app. Using the example above, let us say that you receive sporting updates from another sporting magazine. You are not particularly fond of this magazine'?s content. You can simply block off the content and stop receiving updates from them. This way, you can simply remove content from Twitter accounts you do not like.

4. Twitter is not exactly user friendly when you want to follow a conversation, but Plume, on the other hand, is a lifesaver in this department. Or shall we say Twitter-saver? You can easily follow conversations and know who replied to what comment.

l *The Best Feature*

I enjoy the fact that I can see exactly the kind of content I want to see. The color attribute is an absolute blast. Your eyes are easily drawn to your preferred tweets. You can conveniently recognize the tweets and the users who created them. This allows you to look at the information relevant to you. Perfect for your next business research!

l Twitterrific

Now that you know how to organize content, we have to look at another important factor on Twitter. Twitter, like all other social platforms, functions on the ability to show ads. But what if you do not want to see these ads? What if you want to view your tweets without the ads and promotions?

This is where Twitterrific comes into play. The platform is really convenient when it comes to showing content without a lot of intrusions. You will end up having a seamless experience devoid of interruptions. You will be able to remove those pesky ads and finally focus on absorbing valuable content!

l Benefits of Twitterrific

1. Let us gloss over the basics first. You can compose tweets. You can easily add images along with image descriptions while using the VoiceOver feature. This allows you to use Twitter within Twitterrific without having to switch between two different apps. Using this feature, you will be able to save a lot of time.

2. One of the best features of this app is that you can block promoted content. This means you can view tweets without ads popping up. This is extremely effective when you are looking for plain information. Sometimes, you might be about to tap something and presto! An ad appears and you end up tapping that instead.

3. You can setup multiple windows. This allows you to tap between accounts and easily manage content.

4. The mute button makes it appear yet again! I cannot emphasize how convenient this feature is. Mute all the conversations you do not like.

l The Best Feature

No ads! It practically gives you such a seamless experience on Twitter. Along with the mute feature, you have a near perfect Twitter feed for you. You can view the things you want without any distractions. Now that is what we call a productivity app.

Chapter 7: Productivity Tools for Content Creation and Ideas

Creating content is a challenging task. You, as a small business owner or a freelancer, will know the value of content. It is the part of your marketing strategy that will guide your business, or yourself, forward.

Creating content, however, is not an easy task.

If you are a freelance writer or if you publish an article about your business, then that is a challenge. Coming up with ideas for your article requires a lot of research. You need to be aware of industry trends. You should know the latest news about the topic you are going to write about. If you are a small business owner, you should know more info about similar businesses. If you are someone creating your profile, you need ideas about your niche.

Additionally, once you have found an idea for your content, you need to remain consistent. Consistency requires you to have a long list of ideas ready for use.

But the challenges to creating content do not just end there. Once you have the content, you need to know if they are valuable. You need to check and see if they attract traffic. You need to be aware of their performance on your website or social platforms. If they do not work to bring in audience or traffic, then it is back to the drawing board. Your time gets wasted and you have to start over again. You have to collect ideas once more and create fresh concepts.

The internet is a world of information. A quick Google search can give you tons of information on any topic. While that is important, you need something to organize that information. You should have the power to make connections and draw inspiration from a myriad of sources. You should have the power to choose the information you need and collect them. You should also have the option to grab ideas and find details about them.

All of this is important for content creation and idea generation. Simply discovering information is not enough. It becomes a clutter and your mind will be a mess.

So what can we do in such cases? How can we find a balance between information discovery and information gathering?

To assist you with the task of getting valuable info, you have the below apps. You can use them to store info from the web for later viewing. You can use them to collect important information in one feed. Your task of finding the right information becomes that much easier.

1 Pocket

Remember how we talked about information gathering? You see, you can find news and information from various sources online. You have Twitter and Wikipedia. You even have a host of information sharing websites for you. In fact, as mentioned earlier, you can perform a quick Google search. From there, you can navigate to a number of web pages.

However, you do not necessarily have the time to view all of them at the same time. Imagine going through dozens of web pages. You may not have the time to read the content on all of those sites immediately. You may want to save them for later use. What can you do then?

You use Pocket.

With Pocket, you can save your articles or content and view them at a later time. You might think, isn'?t that the purpose of a bookmark? Well, the benefit of Pocket exceeds towards more than being just a bookmark app.

Here are some of the awesome features of Pocket and their benefits for content.

l Benefits of Pocket

1. When you find articles or content online, you can save them into Pocket. Once you do so, you can view them later and without an internet connection. That'?s right. All the articles you saved can be viewed offline. This means you can navigate to your favorite websites and collect information. You save them to Pocket. You can then open the app and look through your saved articles when you are free. However, as the app saves a simplified version of the page, you may not be able to view the videos on the pages. But the app provides a solution for that as well, as you will see below. Regardless, this is a quick solution to grab your ideas and use them when you are ready.

2. That does not mean you cannot save a video. Through its latest features, the app allows you to save videos as well. Do note that there are content restrictions on videos and, because of this, you may not be able to view them offline.

3. You can add links from all the popular browsers available. Whether you are using Google Chrome or Safari, you can save your content on Pocket. This convenience allows you to work on numerous desktops and mobile devices.

4. All your saved items can be organized. You can create lists to save a particular type of content. Once that is done, you can label the lists the way you would like. You can create as many lists as possible. This way, you can group your ideas for better access. When your mind is ready for one information, you can pull out information for that part.

5. Another awesome feature is the recommended tab. When you feel you have run out of ideas, you need inspiration. Instead of manually performing research, you can use this tab.

Essentially, this tab shows you content similar to the ones you have saved already. For example, if you have been saving content on men's fashion, to find more related content, use the recommended tab. Pocket will then find similar content across the web, from websites to blogs, for men's fashion. This way, you can instantly search and save content for your subject.

6. You need to create content that compliments the convenience of this app. Ideas do not wait. They appear anytime. When they do, and you want to create content, Pocket is there for you. You can easily navigate to your desired information. With that, you can make some awesome content.

l *The Best Feature*

The save feature is excellent. I can easily look for content and save it. Usually, I find myself doing my research during the afternoons and, later, when I have the time to myself, I focus on going through them. However, I have to make a special note to the recommended features. It is so convenient to find more content based on what I like. If I ever need to look for similar content, I know I can do it within the app rather than finding them online. When I may not be able to brainstorm more ideas, Pocket comes to the rescue!

l **Feedly**

So, you now know how to grab information. How about getting them? Sure, you can Google search your way through dozens of websites. As mentioned earlier, you can perform countless Google searches to get the information you want, but where will that get you? Do you even have time to spend on multiple searches? In this situation, you may just wish you could get all the information in one platform. You may wish that you could simply choose your topic or search criteria, and then the information is right there. Who says that is not possible?

Meet Feedly.

With Feedly, you can aggregate all information into a single app. This makes it convenient for you to browse through inspiration and content. The app itself takes information from multiple sources, and it uses top ranking websites and blogs to bring you the content you need. By choosing your topic of focus, you can find your content in an easy-to-navigate app.

l Benefits of Feedly

1. You can choose a preferred source of content or, alternatively, a preferred type of content (example: automobile, politics, gaming, etc.). Once you have made your preference, it is all brought together into one, coherent space. This makes it easier for you to stay updated without much navigation.
2. You can browse content from websites, blogs, YouTube, digital publications, and lots more! All the information you require is just a few simple swipes away.
3. Feedly allows you to share your content, as well. With this, you can collaborate with teams and share ideas and inspirations. You can even create shared boards with your friends. This is important when you want a certain group of people to see specific information.
4. This app improves productivity even more. Not only can you share content with friends, but workflow platforms, too. You can share information to Trello and Slack, to name a few.

l The Best Feature

When you can share information easily with friends, you have a winning app. This is particularly useful when you are working with a team. You and your team can look for information together. When you find something important, you can share it with your team; your team, in turn, can share their information with you. This way, everyone gets aligned on the content they should be creating.

Additionally, let us assume that you and your team are brainstorming ideas for content. Each member of your team can have their own feed. Together, by pooling in your resources, you can accumulate a much bigger collection of information.

The fact that you can share this information on workflow platforms makes the app even better. For example, let us assume you are working on Trello. You have assigned tasks to different members of your team. While going through Feedly, you find information that could benefit the team. Using simple controls, you can share the information to any member of your team or the entire team collectively. When one is working on Trello, inspiration is useful to complete tasks in the best way possible. Feedly allows you to work and share information swimmingly.

1 BuzzSumo

Now we have talked about analytic tools for each social platform, but what if you want to focus on all platforms at once? In fact, what about finding all the popular content on the web? This could take hours. This is because you not only have to find content, but you also have to check its popularity with the masses. It would be perfect to have a tool that does just that. In fact, wouldn't it be convenient to simply enter a search criteria and find popular content on the web? Is there a tool for such a purpose? Well, you only need to look at BuzzSumo for that.

1 Benefits of BuzzSumo

1. One of the things about BuzzSumo is that it is not just another analytical tool. You can actually find the high-performing content related to a particular topic in one space. This allows you to monitor content across the social media space. When you begin to monitor content, you get an idea of how you can develop your own. You think about ways to address the trends out there. When you input your search criteria, BuzzSumo analyzes all topics related to the criteria. It measures how much attention these topics are receiving. They could be blogs, articles, websites, or social media platforms. It looks at how many shares and comments the content has received. It measures clicks, if it is a video. Because on all of these factors, you can gain ideas for content.

2. With BuzzSumo, you can get customized notifications for content. This means you can choose what kind of content you need to be aware of instantly. Let us say that you are focusing on Facebook content for five-star hotels. You want to know if some new content is posted there. BuzzSumo can help you with that.

3. You can also receive information about influencers. Who are people following the most based on your search criteria? For example, let'?s assume you have entered travel as your search criteria. BuzzSumo will look at travel-based influencers. It will also look at other influencers who have used travel-related content. Which influencer gets more shares on their social platform? Who gets more conversations going? Who gains more followers due to their content? By analyzing all of this, you will be able to draw inspiration. You can see what others are doing right and utilize that within your own work.

4. Advanced data filtering allows you to find the content you are interested in. You can even remove those that do not matter to you.

5. BuzzSumo allows you to analyze your competitors. If you are a small business, this will be essential to your marketing. If you see your competitor gaining traction, then you need to know why. Is it because they are regular on the platform? Is their content exceptionally good? Do they engage with their audience more? Do they have the right tools for conversations? By using all of these criteria, you can stay one step ahead of your competition. Combine that with the popular content on the web, and you will have ideas to create better substance. This way, you might just overtake your competition's engagement in no time.

6. You can even explore data. This allows you to plan content for a later time and date. This accessibility also allows you to view information offline.

l The Best Feature

I love the idea of filtering the content I want to see. This allows me to keep up-to-date with the content that matters to me. As a content creator, you need that flexibility to manage information. This is important for you as you do not have time to waste. With BuzzSumo, you can bring a world of ideas to you, without all the extras.

Chapter 8: Productivity Tools for Project Management

There is much to be said about managing expectations. When people look at project management, they often think it is such a waste of time. They consider it an unnecessary addition to their already-high expenses.

In reality, without project management, work does not get done properly. It is true, project management requires a larger budget, but think about it this way: How can you guarantee your team and everyone else on board are working towards the project? How can you align your team to the client'?s expectations? How can you ensure everyone completes their tasks well? Who monitors progress and keeps the work on track? To all of these questions, there is one answer. Project management.

A great project management process ensures that budgets, deliverables, and teams achieve goals. By using a convenient project management tool, you can create targets. You can set visions for the team. You can provide assistance wherever required.

Furthermore, any project requires leadership. Without leadership, it becomes a ship without a captain or navigator. If you are managing the projects, then you need to give it direction. Without knowing what your team is doing, you will not know who is doing well. Or alternatively, who is performing poorly.

But knowing about the importance of project management is just one step. The next step is to find tools that can help manage your projects. These tools should not just be the first thing you find online. They have to match your requirements and, at the same time, be user-friendly.

Think about it. You have collected your ideas. You have brought them together and created your project. But now that you are done, what next? Well, now is the time to add an extra layer of productivity. With these apps, you can collaborate with people, check your work, and more. You can ensure you meet all the requirements of your project before you submit it. It is a way of giving you comfort in your work and maintaining the quality of it, as well.

So, let us look at some of these apps.

1 ProofHub

When talking about project management software, we mean something that fits it all. What we intend by that is that the tool should suit a small-scale business, as well as large organizations. Apart from that, you should be able to manage all phases of a project. You should be able to do this from start to finish. Your planning phase should be conducted properly. You should be able to organize teams, materials, and resources. You should then be able to manage your teams and projects. Finally, you should be able to complete all deliverables. Every component of the process is crucial for a successful project. It is similar to the parts of a computer, where every component plays a vital role.

ProofHub gives you that level of control. It is a single platform that brings together managers, team members, and decision makers. When you know all factors are in play, you can complete your projects with minimal issues.

With ProofHub, you can stay on top of your project deliverables and deadlines. Much can be said about this software. It has been gaining quite a name for itself among managers and office teams. You can see this in its achievements. This is true after the fact that it won the Cloudswave Awards 2014 for being the top project management software.

Using this software, you can work across all critical levels of projects. From your planning stages to your organizing stages, you can manage it all on ProofHub.

l Benefits of ProofHub

1. It acts as a centralized system for clients, teams, and contractors to come together and manage their project deliverables. They can share knowledge, create tasks, and easily assign responsibilities.

2. The entire system is easy to use. There is no complicated set-up procedure. The layout is friendly and convenient for first-time users. One of the features I liked was the arrangement of teams. You can create groups for each team based on task or function. These are all arranged in a neat layout that you can easily access.

3. You can get email notifications so you are on top of everything. You can even set up an iOS or Android app for easy accessibility.

4. You can sync calendars to ProofHub. You can bring in information from Outlook, Google Calendar, and more. This is particularly useful when you would like to manage your appointments and meetings. With this feature, you do not have to switch between accounts to get your work done. Simply bring in your deadlines and arrangements into the app. You can effortlessly coordinate with your team and be aware of any upcoming appointments.

5. You have a chat feature, allowing you to instantly communicate with other members.

6. You can create Gantt charts for operational purposes. A Gantt chart is an effective visualization tool for managing projects. You create project tasks and use markers to note down the progress. By using this, you can see the progress of these tasks

compared to the time allotted to each. You can see which tasks are completed on time and which have been finished early. More importantly, you can find out the tasks that are still pending. This allows you to take action and ensure their completion.

7. Events and milestones can be set up, allowing you a quick overview of your tasks.

l The Best Feature

The fact that you can sync calendars is truly useful. With this, you actually have the power to add all your tasks into one platform. This adds more comfort and convenience into your task management process. Imagine you have a whole lot of meetings scheduled. You bring all of that into one platform, making it easier for everyone to collaborate on the tasks.

I also like the Gantt chart feature. I am quite proficient with Gantt charts, but I know many who are not. Regardless, it is a welcomed addition to the app. I recommend getting to know the basics of Gantt charts. It does not take much time and will help you manage projects better. With that, we move on to the next app on our list.

l Slack

The term, "Slack me this information,"? is getting pretty common in the corporate world. If you do not know someone using this app, then you must be aware of its popularity.

When people ask me to explain Slack, there is only one example I can use. Imagine you have WhatsApp created just for you and your team. That'?s right. Bear with me while I explain this further and you will understand what Slack is all about. You have a special WhatsApp type of app for you and your team. In this app, you can create groups for different teams and different members. You can chat privately with any member. You can send files to those members. The best part is that no one outside of your team can enter this app. It literally becomes your workspace communication tool. In fact, you can even use emojis in your communication.

Sounds like a cool app to have, right?

When you have multiple teams working on one project, you need to arrange them. Alternatively, you could have a great deal of people doing a lot of different things. In order to make sure everyone is aligned, you need a common platform. Slack is that platform for you.

l Benefits of Slack

1. Slack provides you with a common channel where teams can collaborate on tasks. You can arrange different teams in different channels.
2. You have public channels where everyone in the channel can view messages.
3. You can even private chat with anyone, should you need to. This allows communication to be convenient in many ways.
4. Files are easy to share with Slack, allowing you to transfer documents instantly. You can share files with someone individually or you can share it with the entire group. This allows you to coordinate between teams and individual members for various tasks.
5. Your conversations are archived. This means you can always read back into your history for more information. This is also convenient when you want to recover a file. Let us assume you had sent across a document file to a team member. You then encounter a problem where you lose data on your device. Using Slack, you can easily retrieve the document you sent

across. Managing history is also convenient when you want to backtrack conversations.

6. Slack provides a search feature, allowing you to find information when you need it. This search feature can be used within a private chat, allowing you to find past conversations and files. You can also use this in group chats or public chats. Through this search feature, you can keep track of all communication.

l The Best Feature

The convenience of creating a common channel is the best feature, according to me. You can create multiple channels as well. Each of these channels can serve a different purpose.

Let me explain with an example. Let's say you have four members in your team. You have Andy, Ben, Cody, and David. Andy and Ben are the content guys. Cody is responsible for graphics. David works on video content, directing and adding effects to videos. You can create a channel called "?Social Media Graphics." In this channel, you can add Andy, Ben, and Cody. The content guys will create the text for the graphics. Cody will handle the rest.

In another channel, you can have Andy, Ben, and David. This is because David might require content for some of the videos. Having the three in one channel allows them to work effectively together.

However, it does not have to end there. You can create another channel for Cody and David. Perhaps Cody might be able to help David with some graphics or image editing.

In such unique ways, you can make sure your team is equipped to get the job done. In each channel, you can have different people participate. This creates an effective system of work. Everyone is informed, and you have a team that works together to get goals accomplished.

l Fleep

There are a lot of messaging apps for business. Fleep is another communication tool you can utilize for your business. But what makes Fleep so different?

It becomes complicated when you have a communication tool and a separate email client. You might find yourself switching between the two frequently. However, what if you could combine a communication tool with your email? Essentially, they are trying to eliminate emails between teams. This allows you to have quick conversations and streamline communication. And the best part is that you have the ability to make emailing easier.

Welcome to the app called Fleep.

l Benefits of Fleep

1. You have the chat feature, giving you access to have conversations fluidly. You can use this chat to communicate with members individually. You can also create a chat room and include certain members of the team. Using this, you can manage tasks and assign projects to teams effectively.
2. You get the option to assign tasks to specific people. Using this feature, you can set specific targets for different members of the team. Since you can also chat with your team members, you can find out about their progress, as well. By combining the task feature of goals with the communication abilities of a chat app, you can manage projects well.
3. Conversations have a file drawer. This allows you to store documents and access them whenever you want.

4. Now, this is all good when you are talking with your fellow colleagues, but what about clients? What if they do not have Fleep? Well, this is where the magic happens. You see, you can simply add their email address to Fleep. With that, you can view and send emails using Fleep solely. You do not have to navigate to your email for this. Essentially, you can combine all your company's communications into one place.

5. Additionally, you can start audio and video calls in groups for free. Through this, you can connect with anyone who does not have the software.

l The Best Feature

Hands down, the integration of email into the chat system is the best feature. With this, you can communicate with your team and your clients in the same place. Work gets done smoother and more streamlined. You eliminate a lot of processes in between.

Let me highlight this with an example. Let us assume you have a team member by the name of John. John is responsible for the operations section. It is his responsibility to make sure stocks are filled regularly. John received an email regarding a particular stock from a client. John can now view this email within Fleep itself. He can notify you about this email. He can share the email with you directly, or chat with you about it. When you know how to handle the client, you can give John a set of instructions. He will communicate the same to the client within the app itself. When done, he can send across the email to the client. With this, every step of the communication process can be conducted within the app itself. You do not require any external services. You simply connect your app to your email server and everything is taken care of. Moreover, you are not constantly distracted by using two different platforms.

1 Zoom

When you need a collaborator, you need Zoom. So far, we have talked about the tools you can use within your company, but there should be a tool where you can bring in clients and customers, too. After all, that would make things easier for you. You might think that such a tool would not be useful for small businesses, but think of it this way. If you have a small supermarket, you probably have a lot of suppliers. This means you may often run promotions in your supermarket. In order for these promotions to run successfully, you need to get together many of your suppliers. You could of course call them individually, or set up meetings, where you would run your promotions by them and explain the benefits.

Or you could use Zoom. With this app, you can bring multiple collaborators onto the same platform. You can create a conference where you include all your suppliers. You can video chat with them. You can explain your promotion to all of them in one go. With this, you can get your promotions, projects, and even small tasks running smoothly. Essentially, this tool provides a secure, easy-to-use platform for messaging and conversations. These conversations can be in an audio or video format. One of its most notable features is the "Zoom Room," which we will cover as we talk about the product.

Let us dive into the product and find out why it is a must-have.

1 Benefits of Zoom

1. With its "Meetings" feature, you can collaborate, train, and provide support. You have the power to easily make audio and video calls. You can use remote screen features for easy accessibility. It makes the whole idea of starting a meeting convenient. The people you can invite to this virtual meeting room can be from anywhere in the world. This can be a useful

feature if outsourcing your job. If you are a freelancer, you can invite clients to this platform. It will allow you to better communicate and organize your tasks with them. You can set up meetings with numerous people, possibly inviting both your clients and your suppliers. You can have interviews or meetings on the app.

2. With its video webinar, you can bring in up to 100 people into a conversation. This means you do not have to worry about how many people can be invited into a conference. A hundred people is a lot! It also provides nearly 100,000 viewing participants. These people can only view, but not interact. In other words, you can communicate with a hundred people at the same time, however, you can have nearly 100,000 participants. These participants cannot interact with you, but they can be present as viewers. Now, how is this important? Let us say you have a big event coming up. You are going to make a big announcement at this event or possibly even launch a new service. With Zoom, you can invite people to watch the event from the comfort of their home. It allows for a large number of participants and makes the software flexible.

3. With Zoom Rooms, you can remotely collaborate with many teams. You can use a single-touch meeting commencement feature. This is a useful feature to have if you regularly confer with the same people. Instead of having to invite them again and again to the app, you can add them into it. The next time you would like to have a conference, you can do it with one touch. Using this tool, you can create multiple teams for conferences. Let us take the example of the supermarket again. Let's say you bring in your finest oranges from New Zealand. You bring in chocolates from Switzerland. You also bring in the best coffee from India. It must be difficult to get everyone

together, yet each of the teams will have their own access. This way, you simply just notify the team in New Zealand and you can all have a conference immediately. You do not have to invite each member of the team individually. The same goes for the team in Switzerland and India. Using this feature, you can conveniently schedule your meetings. You can create a team and engage through audio and video conferences. The idea is to create a fine combination of conferencing and task management.

l The Best Feature

When you can bring in up to 100 people to participate in a conversation, you have a winning app. You can collaborate with teams within the same city, as well. If you have a group of content writers, you can conference with them easily. As soon as that meeting is done, you can move on to the next meeting instantly. This feature is essential when you want to communicate projects right away. It removes downtime considerably. You have teams collaborating effortlessly. Your clients are able to form immediate discussions and meetings. Conferences are done through simple video calls, as well as additional features. The whole idea is fantastic and adds so much convenience.

l GoToMeetings

Web conferencing is a handy feature to have. When you think about conferencing, however, you might also think about needing an easy-to-use solution. For that reason, you have GoToMeetings. This tool is known for providing exceptional audio and video capabilities. You can use this tool for various purposes, including talking with your customers. Let's say you have a new gadget in your store. A customer would like to take a look at it, but does not have the time to come to your store. In that case, you and the customer can simply boot up the software. Then you can show the product to the customer in a high-quality video setting.

But what makes this tool special? For one, it adds in a scheduling feature. This allows you to keep track of meetings, tasks, engagements, and even project statuses. With this functionality, you can easily keep everything organized in one place. And with that handy feature, you need a handy tool to support it, and so we will be looking at GoToMeetings, a conference platform that is simple and efficient.

l Benefits of GoToMeetings

1. The user interface is easy to use and really convenient. You have people who can jump in on the software and begin using it immediately. Training does not take too long. Adapting to the software is seamless.
2. You can schedule audio calls with either one person or multiple people. This allows you to manage conferences using high-quality audio capabilities. This becomes particularly useful when you do not have the bandwidth for video calls.
3. You can also record conferences. This allows you to have a copy of the meeting, should the meeting involve sensitive topics. This feature is useful when you wish to check back on information later.
4. The idea of creating a custom URL you can share with participants is a welcome feature. This makes it easier for you to invite those you truly want in the meeting. Using this feature, only those who have the URL are able to enter the room.
5. You can also share your desktop screen with the rest of the members in a conference. This is useful when you have something complex to explain. Let us assume you are a freelancer who is working on a client'?s website. You are trying

to explain to them why something does not work the way it should. Instead of giving them detailed explanations, simply share your screen. This way, you can show them what you mean instead of verbally describing what to do.

6. People can join in the meetings using their tablets and smartphones. Conversations can happen instantly as setting up a conference is simple.

7. With its range of international features, you can set up international conferences smoothly.

8. Its "One-Click Meeting" feature saves time and creates meetings instantly.

9. Using a PIN code, you can keep your conferences secure.

l *The Best Feature*

In this day and age, accessibility is key. When you can use both mobile devices and desktop devices, you have a winner. Through this, it is easier to collaborate with teams. It is easier to set up meetings and schedules. You have a convenient tool for all-purpose, international task management.

Chapter 9: Productivity Tools for Time Management and Scheduling

There is no denying it. Time is money. Time is also not on our side. Every moment lost to us is an opportunity gained by someone else. In today'?s world, we are connected in a number of ways. We just spoke about Facebook, Twitter, and Instagram. These three platforms give you a level of connectivity that is unparalleled.

With good time management capabilities, you will be able to accomplish a lot. You can achieve these accomplishments in a relatively shorter period of time. This means you generate more output within a specific period of time.

Let's face it. We all have the same 24 hours as everyone on this planet, but how can we effectively use *ours*? What can we do to make sure we create more profit and revenue within every coming 24 hours?

Additionally, when you learn to manage time, you learn to do things effectively. Instead of jumping from one task to another, you can give each task a different time allotment. For example, you can assign an hour and a half for checking emails in the morning. Then, you can move on to researching your competitors. After that, you can allot a specific amount of time to work on your projects. Finally, you can give yourself time for reports. You will not be able to complete all of this, however, if you are not aware of time. Without management, you may spend too much time on some tasks and too little on others.

Plus, let us not forget the fact that we can get distracted easily. Facebook is a useful tool for marketing, but that does not mean it cannot distract you. It might seem trivial. After all, you just need a quick five-minute break to check your feed. It won'?t take long.

However, before you know it, you are browsing away without awareness of how much time you have actually just spent.

But how can one save time and find ways to work efficiently? Well, you use certain time management and scheduling tools. With these tools, you are aware of everyone'?s tasks. You keep them within a certain deadline.

Time to check out some of these tools.

1 Toggl

If you are a freelancer, then projects work on a time basis. This means you have deadlines to meet. Of course, the convenience of working as a freelancer comes with the downside of being held accountable for any distractions. This affects your workflow. You might underestimate the time required for a task. By the time you get around to doing it, it is already too late! Now you are in panic mode! How can you finish all of your tasks in such a short amount of time?! When you are in need of a time-tracking software for small businesses and freelancers, you have Toogl. With this, you can easily manage tasks within a specific time. Let us look at its many features and benefits.

1 Benefits of Toggl

1. It keeps reminding you of your tasks. With tracking reminders, you will never be allowed to forget your tasks. This works well when you have multiple tasks to take care of, or you have set yourself a deadline. For example, let'?s say you are working on a 500-word report. You have told yourself that you aim to finish the report in four hours. You can set yourself a reminder after two hours so you get a notification. This way, you know that two hours have passed and if you may need to speed things up. This also works when you have

multiple ideas. If you are working on one idea, then you can set a reminder for another idea. This way, you are not easily distracted with one idea before moving on to the next.

2. You have a reporting feature through which you can generate the reports of your activities. As a freelancer, if you are working on a timely basis, then this feature will benefit you greatly. Simply time your sessions. When you have completed your project, generate a report to show how much time you have worked. You can add more details to the report. This will give the client a thorough rundown of your project.

3. You can record how much you use your computer. This is important as you need to know how much time you spend on tasks. Additionally, this is a health concern. You need to give yourself breaks whenever possible. You can set reminders when you have the tendency to use the computer for long periods of time. We often get involved in our work and do not notice the effects it has on our body. With timed reminders, you can give your eyes a break and return to the task at hand. Additionally, when you find out how much time you spend on the computer, you can note your performance. Did you really need seven hours of computer usage for that task? Were you distracted along the way?

4. User groups can be created to segregate teams into different categories. This means that if you are working with teams, you can see how each member performs. This also allows you to monitor the time taken by other members to complete their tasks.

l The Best Feature

The idea that you can monitor your computer usage is wonderful. You can check how much time you spend on social platforms. For example, if you find yourself getting distracted quite often, Toggl can help contain that. With a lot of features, you can stay focused on your work at all times.

l Harvest

Harvest functions in a similar manner to that of Toggl. However, a few features set this tool apart. When you need to know your team'?s time management abilities, you need Harvest. In essence, you can get to know how your team spends their time at work. Its time tracking features are splendid and it even throws in additional features, too.

Let us talk about them and their benefits.

l Benefits of Harvest

1. It makes you certain of your time. Using its time tracker, you can turn your hours into billable time. You can send invoices to clients or employers. This makes it easy for the team to know the time spent on their work.
2. Tracking time may not be easy for everyone, however, with Harvest, you get a lot of options. You can track time at the end of the week or you can keep a constant reminder every day. Whichever method is most convenient, you can use that. For example, you may not want to be reminded about your usage every hour or every day. In that case, you can create a report at the end of the week. A visual representation will show you the time you have spent on your device.
3. You can turn your timesheets into visuals. This allows you to know how much time your team has spent during a week, or even a day.

l The Best Feature

When you can allow your team to manage time their way, you are creating convenience. This increases productivity. That is something I like, and it is by far the best feature of this software.

When you create this level of accountability, teams will be able to take responsibility for their time. This means they begin to work efficiently. Moreover, you can watch your teams and give them feedback whenever required.

l Paymo

When you are in the market for a project management app, then you can do with Paymo. With this app, small-scale businesses can easily manage their projects from start to finish.

l Benefits of Paymo

1. It is ideal for small businesses. You have the feature to collaborate on a lot of tasks.
2. Effective communication allows you to stay in touch with your team members. The chat feature adds an extra level of functionality.
3. Apart from the above, you can easily track time. Time tracked can be converted into spreadsheets.
4. When you are in need of resources, you can add in a reminder to retrieve them. This gives your team a notification, allowing them to understand what they should do.
5. You can easily break your complex tasks into smaller ones. If you are a local business owner, this is useful to create simplicity and attainability.
6. You can join a community of over 100,000 users from around the world. This allows you to communicate with people in 18 different languages. Through this, you can always seek help

and support anytime.

l The Best Feature

The idea that you can create smaller chunks of bigger tasks is satisfying. You have everything you need in order to make your small business task management a real success.

l Everhour

When you need people to stick to time schedules, Everhour is your app. Essentially, you can check on your team'?s time management skills. You can record their work time and this can be used as billable hours. Let us dive into its features and benefits.

l Benefits of Everhour

1. You have a live dashboard for easy navigation.
2. Track project times and record time spent by teams on certain tasks. This allows you to control their efficiency better.
3. You receive real-time notifications. These notifications can be adjusted and used in the manner you wish.
4. To-do lists can be created and aligned with your time.
5. You can estimate project times based on historical data.
6. With complete control over workflow management, you have an awesome level of control.

l The Best Feature

Tracking project times is tricky. This is because you have a lot of tasks and subtasks. Each one has its own time constraints. However, with Everhour, you have an effective system for time management and improvements.

l Time Doctor

Want to know if your team is productive? Then you need to call in the doctor! Let us look at why this online platform is gaining popularity, and then we will get into its benefits.

l Features and Benefits

1. You can easily create time-management schedules for anywhere from 20 to 500 employees.
2. While this may seem like it is made for large organizations, it is suitable for all companies of all sizes. Small-scale businesses can utilize this platform to their benefit as effectively as large-scale ones.
3. It provides real-time tracking facilities, keeping you informed on working hours.
4. You have the ability to set reminders, should you have to inform your team.
5. You have reporting tools to give you an overview of the progress so far.

l The Best Feature

Having the power to keep real-time tracking is superb. Not having to wait for results is a convenience in itself. You can simply hop in and begin monitoring.

Chapter 10: Productivity Tools for Group Document Sharing

When you are working with documents, sharing them can be a hassle. You have emails, of course, and they may not send across large files. For that reason, having a separate sharing tool will help you better manage your files. You can easily work with files and get them ready for use. Some of the tools on this list will assist you with file sharing.

1 Dropbox

When you are in the process of storing and sharing files, there is no way you do not know of Dropbox. It is one of the most popular tools for sharing files, so let us see why it deserves to be on this list.

1 Benefits of Dropbox

1. Its main benefit is that it offers a lot of storage.
2. Its sharing capabilities are free of charge. This is still unbelievable, but it is true. You can always upgrade it for bigger space, of course.
3. When you decide to edit your file online, anyone with the right access can also edit it. This creates a sense of community and creates room for assistance. You can create teams to edit files, allowing groups to work together.
4. It automatically backs up storage photos.

1 The Best Feature

The fact that you have an unbelievable amount of storage for free is spectacular. Dropbox is convenient and easy to use. You can use it across devices for ease of access.

l Evernote

If you need an efficient note-taking system, you have Evernote. With this tool, you have the ability to view all your notes offline. This allows you to make and store notes conveniently. Its user interface is pleasing and well-designed. Navigating between menus is really convenient and it gives you quick access to your tasks.

l Benefits of Evernote

1. No need to worry about limits with its 10 GB of space for uploading notes. I am not even sure if you need that much!
2. Each note can be up to 200 MB, allowing you to create colorful notes and presentations. This is useful when you have to compile a large amount of information in one go.
3. Using Evernote's camera, you can scan your business card and store it on the platform. This is ideal when you need your card in a pinch.
4. Evernote allows you to record audio and add videos to your notes. You can draw on them and combine it with images. Your note is your idea zone. You can design it however you would like.
5. You can create a sign using Evernote, then copy that sign and paste it in documents virtually.
6. This might be a small addition, but the note-maker is a fluid system. It opens quickly and lets you start working immediately. This speed and ease-of-access is something many find convenient, especially those who have a busy day.

l The Best Feature

An offline tool that also allows you to create presentations? Sign us up, we say! There is so much to like about Evernote, but my favorite feature is its space. With 10 GB of space, you have such a voluminous capacity.

l Microsoft OneNote

Making notes is essential in the creative process. You get to visualize your thoughts and come up with strategies based on them. You can alter your current content or create something entirely new. There are tons of things you can do using notes. We have already shown you the cool features of Evernote. Let us now take a look at another note-making platform: Microsoft OneNote.

l Benefits of OneNote

1. Each page of OneNote acts like a paper. You can draw on it. You can add text and images. You can record an audio file and add any information to it. Through this, you can essentially create a scrapbook. As most of the ideas that flow into our heads are in freefall, this app allows us to anchor them.

2. Did you spot something that inspired you? Then simply take a picture of it and add to your OneNote.

3. Does the image have characters in it? Then OneNote can use its text scanning software to identify it. It can search the text online for more information. For example, let'?s say you took a picture of a sign. The sign has a combination of letters and numbers. OneNote can identify those characters and perform a search online so that you can get a better understanding of its meaning.

4. You can also extract text from an image and paste it elsewhere. This is important if you take pictures of business cards or have images featuring phone numbers. Instead of manually entering numbers, simply copy the text and save the number.

5. You can arrange tags for each note you make. When you create plenty of notes, tags can help you to find a specific note you may be looking for. You can have multiple tags based on your preference.

6. You can sync the app with your colleagues. This allows you to share notes and information with people easily. This is particularly useful when collaborating with teams.

7. Since it is a Microsoft product, you can sync it with other Microsoft products, as well. You can create meetings in Outlook and add those to OneNote. Got a Word document? No problem. Add that to OneNote, as well.

l The Best Feature

Imagine having an image. You see a text on it. How can you extract the information? Well, OneNote gives you that capability. It is a brilliant addition to a software that already packs a punch. You have the ability to add names and numbers from business cards. You can have an image of a book and then copy the name of the book. The options are endless. The usage, however, is entirely up to you.

l Simplenote

I think it is time to introduce one more note-making system before you move on. This is another simple note-making system. It allows you to add your files, media, and information in many ways. You can sync this with other devices for free. When you are done taking notes, you can share them with whomever you would like.

l Benefits of Simplenote

1. You can access your files anywhere. Sync it with another mobile phone or PC. You can even access it via a web browser.

This ease of access allows you to reach your notes anywhere, anytime.

2. Not sure if your device is a safe place for keeping notes? Back up your files so you can retrieve them later.

3. Anytime you type something, the note saves your progress instantly. This allows you to search through your other notes without fearing deleted work.

4. Keeping your notes secure is key. With Simplenote, you can encrypt your notes so they cannot be opened by anyone else. This is particularly useful for business owners who keep sensitive information on their devices.

l The Best Feature

The security of course! The ability to encrypt our data means we do not have to worry about anyone seeing it. Even if someone has our phone, we can rest assured that our information stays ours. Encryption works for other purposes, as well. For example, when working with a team, you can allow people access to work on the notes. This tool lets you share your information with those you want.

Chapter 11: Productivity Tools for Boosting Focus and Eliminating Distractions

Sometimes, you may not always have the right focus needed for a task. You may find yourself getting distracted. Oftentimes, your focus might meander to other things. Your musings might interrupt your thoughts. Whatever the case may be, sometimes you just need something to jolt you back to work. You need to be removed from your reverie.

For that reason, we have these exemplary tools to help you out.

1 Freedom

Think about this scenario: You are working on something, but you suddenly feel the urge to check Facebook. You might just need to watch that one video on YouTube. It won'?t take long. It is just a quick 5-minute break anyways. Or perhaps just a single Tweet on Twitter for the day. Maybe it is just one more image on Instagram.

These distractions can be expensive as your productivity lowers. This leads to less output and costly processes.

For this reason, you have Freedom. This tool blocks off unwanted distractions, such as websites, apps, and more, to keep you focused.

l Benefits of Freedom

1. You can block websites that distract you. Want to keep away from Facebook and YouTube? Block them for some time. Keep a set timer on your blocks, so they can be accessed later.
2. Apps on your phone a distraction? The mobile version helps you keep away from them. Keep them locked away until you

are ready to use them.

3. Block the whole internet if you would like to. This is especially useful when you want to work offline. Keep it locked away while you are completely focused on your task at hand.

4. You can keep a whitelist. This means you can make exceptions to websites and apps. Let us suppose your internet is blocked, however, you may need Wikipedia or Britannica to access information. You can do this easily with the use of Freedom.

5. You can also create a blocklist across devices. This way, you will be kept away from your PC and your mobile devices, as well.

l The Best Feature

The ability to create a blocklist is a feature you will appreciate. You can make exceptions, block multiple devices, and even create block schedules. All of this will create an efficient focus system where you can get more accomplished.

l Self Control

One of the reasons you should consider Self Control is because of its simplicity. Essentially, Self Control is a time-management tool that allows you to focus better on your work. You can restrict access to certain websites and apps for a certain period of time, yet its effectiveness lies in its ease-of-use.

l Benefits of Self Control

1. Simply boot up the app, choose your time, add your website, and you are done. It is that simple. This is what makes this app great to use if you are in a hurry.

2. You can create a list of websites you want whitelisted. These can be saved on the app and imported later. The app itself also

gives you recommendations for websites you can use.

3. You can receive a list of blacklisted websites from the app. These include publications, entertainment, and other recommendations.

4. One thing that makes Self Control unique is that it is an open source project. This way, anyone is free to make changes to it. It allows users to make adjustments to it from all over the world.

5. You can keep the app icon floating above all windows. This allows you to easily access the app and make changes to it whenever needed.

l The Best Feature

Open source gives people across the globe the chance to work on a project. This means there could be developers out there with more skills who can easily access the project files. With these, they can continue making improvements to the app. With this feature, you can be sure there are constant updates.

l Focus Booster

When you want to create timed sessions for your work, Focus Booster might just be able to help you with that. This app is based on the Pomodoro technique. Here, you work for 25 minutes straight and then take a 5-minute break. Using this strategy, you can get more work done in a shorter period of time.

l Benefits of Focus Booster

1. It is ideal for freelancers. You can continue working for bursts of 30 to 40 minutes. Then you can take a quick break and return to your work. This has been known to raise

productivity considerably.

2. Alternatively, you can opt to remove this feature and create your own schedule.

3. Writers will find that this technique works brilliantly for them. It allows them to use their creativity to the fullest. Then, they can take a break and return to their work with a fresh mindset.

4. If you would like, you can utilize The Rule of 52 and 17. With this, you would work for 52 minutes, followed by a 17-minute break.

5. Whatever your preference, this tool works to enhance your work.

6. You can also create a report. This will use your time as billable hours. If you are working with clients, you can show them your work time. The app is spectacular if you are doing remote jobs or freelancing.

l The Best Feature

The modes of working with this app are amazing. You can choose the mode you would like to work with. This app is meant to give you the most convenient way to generate more output. Whatever method you use, you can always try it out before sticking to it.

l Forest

There is a sense of accomplishment when you use Forest. You feel like you want to do more. This is probably because of the idea of growing a tree. You see, every time you work without getting distracted, your virtual tree grows. If not, your tree dies instantly. They do not give you any options for reversing its death.

This is the basic setting behind Forest.

You create a time for yourself. If you stick to that time, your tree grows. If you get distracted and use your phone or another app, your tree dies.

l Benefits of Forest

1. The app is intuitive and beautiful. The thematic idea of growing a tree is clever. It is a symbolic representation of your own work. If you are doing well, your work grows. If not, it just fades away.
2. Every time you plant a tree, you will be adding to your forest. In the end, you are presented with a beautiful little patch of trees and vegetation. This is visually striking and acts as a morale booster.
3. You have a number of settings you can use. Just to name a few, you can keep the screen on while the app is functioning, or you can turn on sound notifications for your forest'?s status.

l The Best Feature

The entire design and idea of the app is ingenious. It works well to motivate you. It is visually appealing and makes you feel like you are in a state of meditation. There is an urge to do more. You feel like you are constantly waiting for the next opportunity to grow your tree. Eventually, this is what we need, an app to help you focus and improve your productivity.

l Brain.fm

Brain.fm has a unique approach to productivity. It involves music. The app uses a select collection of audio tracks. According to the app, these tracks are backed by science. With this music, you can improve your focus and enhance productivity.

l Benefits of Brain.fm

1. With scientifically proven methods, you could soon find yourself in deep focus. The music has been researched and composed for specific means.
2. You can choose your objective, and Brain.fm will give you the right music. You can even set a timer. This way, you can decide how long you would like to play the music for.
3. This app can also be used for sleep and relaxation. Simply choose the option for sleep and you will have a selected playlist.
4. You can even pick a certain type of music if you do not like the one you are listening to. With these options, you can create a personal space for work, sleep, and relaxation.

l The Best Feature

I enjoy the fact that developers try to add more into their apps these days. With Brain.fm, it gives you the flexibility to use it for what you want it for. You can use it for focusing on your work, should you require it. If you are under a lot of stress, the app can help you with that as well.

Whatever the case may be, you have a lot of options.

l Productivity and Social Media

If you are working on social media marketing, you will need to remain focused. This is because you are working with a lot of elements. You need to brainstorm ideas and maintain schedules. You will be working with insights and social media advertisements.

However, as we have mentioned about productivity apps, a lot of you may have questions about social media marketing itself. For that reason, I am going to give you a quick overview of social media and online marketing.

1 FAQs on Social Media Marketing

There are some questions on the topic that need to be asked and answered in order to understand it better. Here are some different questions:

Is social media effective?

Yes. Social media is a great tool you can use to promote your products and services. Social media is one of the most widely used marketing tools in the world. This is due to its ease of use and reach. You can effortlessly reach out to a large number of people by marketing through social media. As you know, millions of people use social media, and you can easily communicate with all of them. Think of it as being able to put up a billboard to advertise your business for free on the busiest freeway in the world. Everybody will have a look at it and try to connect with your company in one way or another.

Should I invest money in it?

No. You need not invest any money in it. No social media will expect you to pay money to market your products. Even if money is involved, then it will be very little—?like buying paid ads. If someone is trying to solicit money from you and citing social media as the reason, then you should not pay any money. You should be careful and do all the advertising by yourself.

Should I be socially active?

No. You need not be socially active to advertise online for your company. You can start from scratch and be able to reach out to many people. Being socially active or inactive is not a criterion that will affect your success in social media marketing. You can get someone to advertise for you and find success with that. You can also learn everything you need within a month or so and start advertising online.

Social media marketing is not rocket science. You can establish a business by understanding and utilizing the basics.

Who should I employ?

If you wish to employ someone to look into your social media marketing, then pick those who are socially active. You should also choose someone who is up for a challenge. This is because whomever you hire should be able to understand the preferences of your target group and cater to them specifically. They should also have enough free time and be available at all times to update your pages. Not only that, but they must also be up for the task of informing people about any new products and services.

Can old companies start social media?

Yes. It doesn't matter whether you are a new company or an old one. Old companies can also come up with new strategies to promote their products and services. In fact, if you are already an established company, then people will be able to recognize your brand, which will work in your favor.

How do I check progress?

It is quite easy to check your progress with social media. All you have to do is look at the change in the number of customers. That will tell you how much social media has helped you. You will experience elevated sales and sell many products and services within a short period of time, which will help tell you how much progress you have made. If you really want to be sure of it, then you can maintain a journal. You can look at how many people have visited your site and see how many of those have been converted into customers. You can avail the help of a tracker to check for the same.

Can I reboot the strategies?

Yes. In fact, it is important for you to reboot strategies from time to time. There is no point in having the same strategy for a long time. You have to change it up every now and then and aim to appeal to as many new people as possible. You can make use of a temporary strategy and change it seasonally. If you think a change is requisite, then you should go for it. Your team will be able to handle this aspect well.

Are the choices limited to just these mentioned above?

No. There are many other choices to pick from, like Google+ and LinkedIn. Once you get accustomed to these and come up with winning strategies, you can turn to the others. The point is to advertise your company and its products on as many different platforms as possible. This is to make sure you get noticed.

1 Social Media Marketing Dos and Don'ts

There are many dos and don'ts of social media marketing you must understand, and they are as follows:

Dos

Do Plan

It is extremely important to plan everything out in life. This is especially true for those trying to advertise on social media. If you are planning on promoting your products and services on social media, then you must start with a plan. This plan should tell you how to go about the marketing process and when to do what. If you don't have a plan, then you are bound to get lost like a tourist in an unknown country. You can come up with the plan by yourself or work with a team. Once the plan is ready, you and your team can start implementing it.

Do Diversify

It is extremely important for you to diversify your strategy. Don'?t keep doing the same things over and over again. Keep it as diverse and interesting as possible. You have to change things up regularly and appeal to your audience. You should also diversify the content on the various sites. Plastering the same old thing everywhere will make it boring for your audience. The strategies you pick for the different sites should stick with the platform. They should reach out to that specific audience.

Do Recycle Content

You can recycle the content from time to time. This means you can make use of content that has already been used, yet with a twist. This is especially important for all those who are short on time and look to finish their update early. However, don't make the mistake of simply copying and pasting the content as it is. You have to change it a little and make it look fresh. You have to change the elements and tailor it to cover the new topic. Recycling is fine as long as you know how to do it right.

Do Reply

You have to reply to your customers' queries and listen to what they are saying. Don't indulge in fighting with people who are just trying to annoy you. You have to reply to each and every customer, if possible, and keep them involved. Replying to customers and getting their opinions is extremely important. You have to listen to what they are saying and make any necessary changes. After all, your customers are the most important part of your business. You have to keep them as happy as possible if you wish for your company to make steady progress.

Do Announce

You have to make due announcements on your social media sites. You have to keep your audience informed and let them know about everything going on in your company. Not telling your customers about what's new will leave them uninformed and affect your sales. You have to be proactive and tell them everything in advance. You have to use your social media platform in every way to appeal to a large audience. Only then will you be able to find success.

Don'ts

There are many don'ts of social media marketing you have to consider, and they are as follows:

Don't Copy Strategies

It is extremely important that you don't copy strategies from your competitors. You have to remain as independent and unique as possible. You need to do things that will work in your favor. If you copy strategies, you will end up hurting your own business. You have to pick strategies that will work best for your company specifically. Remember to keep changing them from time to time. Also, remember that people's tastes and preferences keep changing and so should your strategies.

Don't Be Boring

Don't make the mistake of being boring, as you will start to lose your audience. You have to keep it as fun and exciting for them as possible and only then will you be able to contain them. If you are giving them some boring recycled content and expect them to stick around, you will be disappointed. You can turn to many sources for inspiration. You can even incorporate some of their characteristics into your advertising and marketing campaigns.

Don't Employ Random People

You have to avoid employing random people who are not right for your company. You have to look into their background and check to see if they will be a right fit for your company. If you employ the wrong people, they will end up hurting your company. Once you find the right kind of people, you will have to test them. You have to try to pick a diverse group of people to work for you. Some young, some older, and some who are well-experienced for this type of job.

Don't Be Erratic

Most customers expect their favorite companies to be predictable. This means they will like you even more if you are punctual and provide timely updates. You have to put yourself in your customers' shoes and plan everything out. Would you not prefer that a company you like updates their Facebook status at the same time every day? Similarly, you have to think about your customers' reactions when they see the new update at the same time. You have to instruct your team on how to go about this and get them to update the sites regularly.

Don't Ignore Marginal Customers

You should never ignore any customer. You never know when one of them will prove to be your most valuable customer. It is easy to find which customers are proving to be your best. You have to try to treat everyone equally rather than sidelining the latter. One might suddenly become your best customer and bring in many others.

1 Social Media Exclusive Strategies

Reaching Out

One of the most important aspects of sales is being there for the customer after the sale is over. You have to allow them to reach out to you. That is only possible if you provide them with contact information. One good way of getting your customers to notice your online campaigns is by telling them to contact you. You have to tell them that you can be reached by finding your number on your Facebook page. This is sure to get many people visiting your Facebook page. Similarly, you have to work towards promoting all your different social media platforms.

Online Only

Many people find it extremely alluring to find online exclusives. Remember that everybody wants something different and a cut above the rest. They will be interested in buying things others may not own. You can offer it to them through your social media platform, as they are sure to be happy about it. You have to understand that not all, 100 percent of your audience will access your social media platforms. However, when they spread the word about these exclusive products to others, that number will go up.

Discounts

Who doesn't love discounts? Your social media crowd will be extremely happy if you offer them social media specific discounts. You could announce that they can have a certain percentage off if they like your Facebook page or retweet something. You can also tell them that by clicking on the link of the website, they may obtain X or Y discount. But remember that discounts need to be substantial and should not just be some random number. You have to aim at something like 10 or 15 percent, and only then will they be interested in it.

Reward Points

You can start a rewards point system. This means that you offer your customers unique reward points. Using these, they can redeem them by accessing your website through your social media websites. The points will add up and allow them to get something for free after a certain amount is reached. You have to make an announcement about the same and generate interest among them. Remember, though, you have to offer them something good in terms of the points and rewards.

Referral Rewards

You can also offer your customers referral rewards. This means that you offer those who introduce new customers to your site a certain discount with your company. This will help them remain inspired to bring in more people. This will work both ways as you will attain a bigger customer base. Here, too, you have to pick a big discount to offer.

Affiliates

It pays to associate with other companies similar to yours and offer your customers unique discounts. You could tell them that by buying from your company rather than another company, it will help them win discount coupons. They can then use these to buy products from the other company, as well. This will also help you get noticed by customers who follow the other company. They, too, will advertise and tell their customers that shopping from you will give them a discount. You have to announce it to your audience in order for them to know about it. Keep in mind that you should partner up with a company that has plenty of customers.

Contests

You can announce contests on your social media page and get people to take notice. These contests can be anything. You can also ask them to take interesting pictures of themselves using your products and then share it with you. As a reward, you should announce interesting gifts and prizes they could win. They will be motivated to continue being a customer only if they like the reward you have to offer.

New Products

You can make your social media platform a place to announce your next line of products. People will be interested in knowing what you have to offer next. They will visit your social media sites to find out about it. Because of this, you have to help them form a habit of visiting your social media page often. You could have them download a brochure announcing the products.

Online-Only Events

It is a good idea to hold events for your customers. You can invite all your online customers to attend the event and help them get to know one another. You will have to ask them to leave feedback so that you can work on your marketing strategy. You should also ask them to bring along other people who could be potential customers.

These points above form the different things you can do to promote your social media sites, but it's not limited to just these. You have to do other things that will help bring in focus.

The 80/20 Analysis

The 80/20 Analysis is a type of analysis to help understand which site is bringing in most customers.

It is a fairly simple mathematical calculation that will tell you which site is working for you and which one isn't. You have to start by looking at the total number of people you have across all your social networking sites. Add them. Now, write down the names of the individual sites on one side of the column. Add their respective number of people in the next column. Divide each with the total, and you will have your final numbers. Here, the one that has the lowest number is your best site, and the one with the highest is not doing all too well. You have to work on the latter site to increase its value to your business.

You can use the same analysis to find the best customers, the best products, and so on. It is best to take a mathematical route. This will give you an accurate result and help you find the best amongst all your options.

1 Use SMART Goals

Setting clear goals for yourself will help to motivate you to follow through on them. When it comes to choosing the right goals, ensuring the ones you choose are SMART is always a good choice.

Specific: Good goals are specific, which means you want to be sure the goal you choose is extremely clear. Keeping specific goals in mind will instead make it much easier for you to go ahead with them. You can power through whatever task you are currently undertaking.

Measured: You want the goal you ultimately decide on to be one where progress can easily be measured. This will assist you to stay on track throughout the entire process. It will also make any changes easier to attain.

Attainable: SMART goals are those that are attainable given a realistic amount of effort. You should not put yourself in a situation where a large group is focused exclusively on you at first. Instead, a better choice would be to set an attainable goal, such as making five conversions in one week. It is important that you do not lean too far into the other direction. This direction is one where you pick something you can do without any real effort. Goals that are too easily attainable won't do anything to improve your social media marketing.

Relevant: It is important that the goal you choose is relevant to your current situation. Relevance is key to turning the SMART goal system from a one-time thing into a pattern. Remember, you want these early goals to be as meaningful as possible.

Timely: SMART goals are those that have a clear deadline attached. Goals without a clear timeframe for completion are goals that are less likely to ever be completed. Without a clear timetable, you can easily push away what you know you need to do until the end of time. Setting a timeframe will force you to confront what it is you want to do. The timeframe you choose should be enough to make you hustle, but it doesn't need to be so tight to the point of being unrealistic.

Conclusion

Thank you for reading *Social Media Marketing Productivity Hacks*! This book was written to support you in understanding the various key social media tools you need to know about going into 2019, 2020, and beyond. You need to know how to use them, understand time management skills, and learn about communication software. I hope you were able to gain everything you needed to know in order to start building strategies online.

Remember, the most effective strategy you can enforce is the use of the right tool. It is not effective to jump onto several tools and spread yourself thin. This will cause you to struggle to generate a presence for your brand. If you want to generate a positive presence, you need to focus on just one or two platforms at first. Then, you can add one or two more as you go. It is best to have a larger, more productive presence on just one platform.

Now that you have read this book, you will want to make sure you verify your productivity tool requirements. Start using those tools that are going to serve you most in achieving those goals. Make sure you start with the one best aligned with your company. Give yourself time to adapt to its learning curve. Ensure that you start generating productivity from it in a relatively quick manner. That way, your productivity is effective and worthwhile in the long run.

Lastly, if you enjoyed this book and felt like it has supported you, then please take the time to review it. Your honest feedback would be greatly appreciated as it will help me generate more great content for you!